CASTING

The Art of Divining by Objects

& Figures

Ash William Mills

Frist published Bealtainn (May) 2022 By Scottish Cunning Ways. All rights reserved.

No part of this booklet may be reproduced, stored in a retrieval system, or transmitted in any form or by any means, including electronic, mechanical, photocopying, microfilming, recording, or otherwise, without written permission from the author.

All text and images are copyrighted

Text Copyrighted ©2022 by Ash William Mills

Book and Design by Ash William Mills, Edinburgh 2022

Scottish Cunning Ways

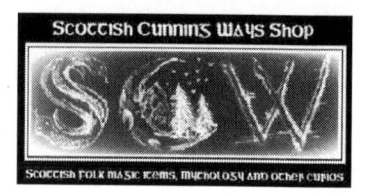

Introduction: *Casting the Lot*

I first became aware of Casting the Lots over 20 years ago when I was seeing people like Mama Starr Cassa casting the bones within American conjure, and I was instantly attracted to this form of divination since I am naturally a visual reader. At this time, I was already reading tarot and tea leaves which I learnt from my great aunt. Casting lots or Cleromancy is one of the oldest forms of divination which although is seen in eastern culture and popularised today, it was also practiced by ancient Europeans.

It seems the method was the practice of throwing down sticks marked with certain figures or signs. In Scandinavia, the method of casting lots is a simple one: they cut a branch from a fruit-bearing tree and divide it into small pieces which they mark with certain distinctive signs and scatter at random onto a white cloth. In ancient Irish mythology, the Gaelic method of Casting the Lots is mentioned in the tale of Dalan and Eochaiod Airem. Dalan who was the druid to Eochaiod, took four rods of Yew wood and wrote Ogham signs (unknown) on them, and by the means in which he threw them down he divined the whereabouts of Eochaiod queen which with Dalan's seership, Eochaiod found that his queen was in Fairyland. If you are interested in this kind of Gaelic Cleromancy then I detail my own version in my first book *The Black Book of Isobel Gowdie and Other Scottish Spells & Charms.*

The Casting of Lots is mentioned in the bible which mentions in the Old Testament of Jews threw down marked sticks and stones in order to divine the will of God:

> Israel cast lots, but not for sport or pleasure or material gain. There were no bets or wagers or stakes, no losses or winnings. It was not done to enrich the temple or the priests or for charity. The lots were used merely to show Jehovah's decision or direction in a matter: "The lot is cast into the lap; but the whole decision is of Jehovah." (Prov. 16:33, Da) It was a means of ending disputes: "The lot puts an end to disputes, and decides between powerful rivals." (Prov. 18:18, AT)

Today, all sorts of different items and objects can be seen used in Casting the Lots such as shells, stones, bones, pieces of jewels etc The method i detail in this booklet is part inspired by American Contour and the Divination Mat, housed in the Museum of Witchcraft and Magic once owned by Bessie Brooks, a local traveller woman in the south-west of England during the 1930's.

Bessie Brooks Divination Mat

One of the interesting pieces of evidence regarding the practice of casting lots is an artefact held at the Museum of Witchcraft and Magic (Cornwall) is the 'Divination Mat' which is a piece of tanned calf skin with symbols painted on in black and is dated some point around the 1930's. The Museum's description of the artefact goes as follows:

> Many wise women in the South West made their predictions from the fall of stones, dried beans or other small objects. These they cast on to lines and symbols marked on the ground, or on a piece of cloth or leather such as this stone casting skin. Original text by Cecil Williamson: "Many witches in the south west (Cornwall)make their predictions from the fall of stones, skulls, dried peas or beans and a host of other objects which may take their fancy. These they cast upon a prepared and patterned area of ground or material. This is a witch's casting skin, covered with crude basic markings and used by a travelling person called Bessie Brooks who worked the farms, markets and pubs throughout the south west in the 1930's."

No one knows just what the symbols mean or how they were interpreted by Bessie Brooks but as a professional guess from my research in folk magic and divination I can try and provide some context to this artefact. Within my method of Casting the Lots, you have dividing grids, in this case it's a square with four lines crossing making eight spaces containing signs and symbols. Firstly, my guess is that the photo of the Divination Mat is pictured in the opposite way around and it looks like it would make sense to have it with the double cross symbol at the top of the mat facing away from you due to how the symbols are positioned. My explanation of the symbols and signs is truly an educated guess and can comments on the means of just a few. The outer symbols of the grid, to each sides contain: two eight-point star-like symbols, a diamond, and a triangle, and each are reversed positioning to each other. Denoting opposing and dual symbology in the. In folklore, the lefthand direction is commonly known as unlucky, negative or the destructive forces, and so, giving that you were looking at it in the angle I suggested, both the left outer symbols might point to negative or positive outcomes in a reading such as the coffin symbol picture (top bottom-left) and the church ((bottom-right).

The coffin obviously represents death and like the death card in Tarot it doesn't necessarily mean a negative or literal sense. It can mean a death of old project, or something needed to let go of to success further in life, so it could possibly mean this in the same interpretation. To the right there is a symbol of what looks like a church and the letter 'S' which represent "sanctified 'or sacred ground. Judging on divination during the 1930 it was still quite popular as it is today also, for the enquire to know when or who they will marry in future by divinatory means. So, this could be interpreted in some way who or when the person, being read for by Bessie when or who they will be wedded. Another symbol which is I can interpret is the symbol which a '4' joined with a square and a curvy line next to it. The 4-like may resemble a apotropaic mark found carved into old building by doorways and roof/ceiling beams as a protections against malevolent forces, and perhaps the square a house and therefore, represents a house well protects by god or some divine power. If so, the curved next and away from it could represent a serpent, the first representation of evil (garden of Eden) in Christian theology and in a whole represent a enquires household status of strength in faith, divine protection, and family order. Other than what I have given a possible explanation into the symbology of the Divination Mat I don't know and will remain a mystery.

As for the symbol at the outer top of the grid, looks like it resembles the Patriarchal Cross or the Cross of Lorraine with two circle each side. This cross is used by Eastern Orthodox churches, so not only gives us a clue to Bessie's religious and ethnic background of Eastern roots and heritage but provides us with a possible meaning of the symbol used in this kind of divinatory practice. In Christian theology, the Patriarchal Cross the top horizonal line represents the death of Jesus Christ, and the second his resurrection. Again, we see two opposition of the natural and supernatural forces of life, and it be centred at the middle-top could represent a neutral or unclear readings of the Divination Mat. The two circles either side of the cross, like the one used in my own casting method, could represent the separation of the Christian symbol 'Vesica Piscis' or double-joined circles. When arranged so that the symbol is horizontal, with its two overlaid circles placed one above the other, it symbolizes the interface between the spiritual and physical worlds, represented by the two circles. Again, duality and opposing symbology!

So, keeping in mind both symbols of the cross and circles similar symbolic representation, I assume that if an object such as stones, skulls and dried peas or beans fell on this symbol, it could mean that the reading or question divined by the enquirer is inconclusive or could denote the reading leading towards a negative aspect in that person's life. Also, like my own casting method, the spaces outside the grid could represent the otherness or outer limits of our existence, and therefore these areas of the Divination Maat could denote something that beyond or hidden the enquirer's knowledge or awareness interpreted by Bessie.

How to use the set

When I first came up with this way of Casting the Lots, I must admit the inspiration came from Bessie Brooks Divination Mat which is why I felt like I needed to mention for that reason as well for historical context into casting lots in Britain. The symbology of the grid itself is sacred to the saltire or cross of St. Andrew, the patron saint of Scotland and many other countries within Europe., and within itself has its associations with divining in Scottish legend.

It is believed that in 832AD an army of Picts under Angus mac Fergus, High King of Alba, and aided by a contingent of Scots led by Eochaidh (Kenneth mac Alpin's grandfather) had been on a punitive raid into Lothian (then and for long afterwards Northumbrian territory) which were being pursued by a larger force of Angles and Saxons under one Athelstan. Before going into battle in Athlestaneford, king Angus being fearing the outcome of the war, led prayers for deliverance, and was rewarded by seeing a cloud formation of a white saltire (the diagonal cross on which St Andrew had been martyred) against a blue sky. The king vowed that if, with the saint's help, he gained the victory, then Andrew would thereafter be the patron saint of Scotland. The Scots did win, and the Saltire became the flag of Scotland.

In this legend of how St. Andrew and his symbolism became the patronage of Scotland, we clearly see associations with divining and omen reading, in this case foretelling the outcome of a war between the Scots and the Angles and Saxons, and it is because of this reason I have used this as the main symbol in the dividing grid in Casting the Lots. Before Casting the lots, as well as calling on my ancestors, I do call on the aid of St. Andrew as the patronage of the Scottish soil I live but I also call on St. Bride for her folk associations with Augury also. However, the symbology of the grid and who you call on to spiritual aid you are completely up to you.

The Prayer for Casting the Lots

I call to my Familiar spirits; ancestors, guides, and angels, shine down upon my cloth,
Questions to be answered, as I cast these objects aloft.
Of bones and stones, strings, and things,
All that fate and destiny brings.
Show me now, in these objects that fall,
ancestors, guides, and angels, hear my call!
-Ash William Mills

Psalm (22:18-19) for Casting Lots

They divide my clothes among them
and cast lots for my garment.
But you, Lord, do not be far from me.
You are my strength; come quickly
to help me.

Other symbology used are related to how the diviner can interpret the divinatory meanings, and then able to read it in the way you do a story. Constating on one quarter of the grid at a time, starting clockwise from the top and connecting each lot or object to how it has fell on the casting cloth. The way in which diviner can use this method of Casting the Lots is complex yet simply once you know the structure and symbology of the lots and casting cloth. With reading the lots and a story, it has a beginning, middle and end. In this case, a reading can indicate life experiences associated in either the past, present and future or simply a series of events being consequences from each other. All which will make sense in next chapters explaining the meaning of each of the lots and symbols, and the examples of a reading interpretation given in this booklet.

Casting the Lots sets can be purchased on my Etsy Store Scottish Cunning Ways, but you can make one I you wish to do so yourself. Also, although I provide information on the Lots used in this booklet/set, there is no problem with you adding or supplementing other objects in Casting the Lots. You can make it as personal as you like. However, I will now explain the meanings of the objects used as the Lots and symbology of the Casting cloth.

The Lots: Objects of Divining

The Key: This can represent new opportunities opening to you, property, or business, or simply a doorway or path that is opening to you. Whether it's a bad path or not!

The Coin: This represents wealth, and it comes in many ways: Wealth in friendships, money, knowledge, business etc

The Bean: This represents growth, whether you are lacking or flourishing in an aspect in your life.

The Wishbone: Represents luck and fortune, whether it be bad or good, such as you might be lucky in dating or unlucky in finding a job.

The Feather: Represents guidance, either a higher power is guiding you in the right direction or you may need guidance in the course of actions you're going or about to take.

The Skulls: The red skull represent yourself; white is your ancestors who guide and aid you, and the black represents other people around you.

The Hand: represents the helping hand and denotes either you are needing to ask for help in something or you are relying on other people too much.

The Jewel: Represents beauty and the material world. It could mean vanity, or you need more confidence in yourself, or it could mean you are focusing on too much of physical things to see the bigger picture. The Divination set that I sell comes with a unique jewel piece.

The Sunflower Seeds: Duality & Opposites. The Sunflower correspondences with the solar powers, it represents abundance, wealth, and Success of all the attributes mentions in the previous Lots. The black and white qualities of the seeds represent the duality and opposing forces in life such as positive & negative effects or situations. Depending on how they fall really does denote the outcome. Odd or even amongst the seeds on each quarter can foretell if the issues in these areas in your life are affecting you negatively or positively, or if the dark or light side of the seeds is facing a sign. Odds & Dark side are negative results and Evens & light is a positive.

The Red Thread represents the very threads of fate and destiny. The thread itself can make a shape or figure which can be divined to whatever object or sign it has landed on. It can also act as "connecting threads" which if wrapped or overlapping one item to another, this can denote a situation or event being connected in the reading.

The Casting Cloth: Predicting the Signs

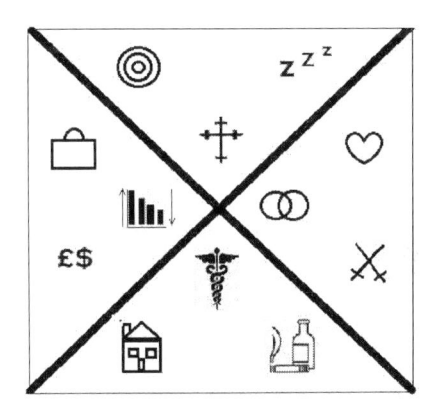

<u>Nothern Quarter: *Triple Circle*: Represents the mind (first circle), body (Second) & Spirit (third) Perhaps you are feeling low right now, feeling stress, anxiety etc or have been very productive in your actions and desires. Depending on where an item has fallen divines the outcome of the reading.

The Cross: represents faith & Belief, this might be to do with your own morals, dignity, or respect. You may lack or have courage in what you do or about to do.

The Triple Z: represents your dreams, desires & aspirations. There might be future goal or life event you are or must strive towards such as a new career, travelling, new project etc or you are lacking in imagination and drive in life right now.

Eastern Quarter: *Love, Relationships, Enemies & Friends*

The Heart: represents your passions, interests & love affairs. Maybe your passionate or disinterested about your business, hobbies/arts, social event etc, or your heart is just not in what situation you are in right now.

The Double Circle: represents relationships & connections. It could be your relationship with family, a partner or child, or unhealthy relationship like that boss at would that has a grudge or negative disposition towards you, and something needs to be done to reconcile that.

The Crossed Swords: Represent confliction & confrontation. It either means two divining forces coming together, opposites attach or the two conflicting matters which don't blend well.

Southern Qaurter: *Social events, Health & Household*

The Bottle & Cigarette: Represent social occasions & Life events. Such as socialising with friends, a business meeting, a wedding etc. This can mean that you need to be socially active, create an event that beneficial to your business or hobby, or it could mean you are spending too much time going out, overspending on your resources, and not focusing on the importance issues in life.

The Healing Sign: represents health and vitality. Health and vitality can come in different ways, not just in physical. It could mean your own bodily health but also healthy friendships, relationships, gardening etc it maybe be that way that you spend your money or save are based on healthy decisions, or an unhealthy relationship which needs work on or to come to an end.

The House: represents truly on your household & the family unit. Such as your Childs, mortgage/rent/bills, maintenance, stability, or instability etc This could mean that all is going well in the home right now and you are on top of things, and in your family, unit is going stable, or it could mean that things need sorting in the home like that leaking roof, your phone bill or reassessing your incoming and out goings.

Western Quarter: *Finance, Abundance/poverty & Work/Career*

The Currency: represents finance & income. Whether your financial comfortable or struggling such as you may have just got a promotion or inheritance which is now benefiting financially, or your job just isn't enough salary and maybe best to look for another job/career.

The Graph: Represents the up's & downs in life. An increasing or decreasing situation or position such as money, relationships, life expectations etc. It may mean that all things are on a positive rise for you right now, the path to success is onwards, or it could mean you have high expectations and maybe looking at more realistic actions or you're spending beyond your means.

The Briefcase: Represents Work, Education & Career. Although these can mean in the literal & physical sense, they can also mean hardship in other areas such as working on your relationships, self-esteem & confidence, ambitions etc. This may mean that the work you are putting into your house is improving its value for sale, or you are lacking the drive or hardship that is necessary to succeed.

Dividers & Borders of the Cloth

Borderlines: Often when the lots or an object land on the bordering lines that divide each quarter means that they are interconnected from one subject/issue to another, or a decision needs to be made between the two such as choosing the right career can benefit your income greatly or choosing overeating over exercise/diet and is causing health problems. For example, for the latter, the feather is overlapping the southern and western borders, and is going from the Healing symbol to the graph, and the red skull is facing down or left, it could mean your eating too many foods which are not good for you and may or is affecting your health.

Overboard: Often when the lots fall on or over the borders of the casting cloth this represents things which are not considered or going unnoticed such advice, upcoming events/occasions, troubles etc This can range from you forgot about valuable object you been meaning to sell for as a bit of temporary finance, or as simple as the heating being on a different setting is the reason for your bill being sky high. This reading denotes knowledge which is unknown or forgotten about which can be either beneficial or harmful for you.

Bearing the Cross: Represents Negative & Positive results. The dark and light crosses denote in the quarters if they are negative or positive outcomes. Black crosses being negative results/outcomes and the light a positive. This really depends on which crosses the Sunflower Seeds fall on. For example, if they land on or near a dark cross in the northern quarter you are lacking in these areas greatly and the opposite if it is a light cross. This is how you can tell if you are succeeding greatly in these areas or need improvement and change.

X Marks the Spot: Represents Unity & Diversity. If the Lots lands on or around the centre of the dividing quarters this denotes that the reading covers a lot of life situations and events at once, and/or that there several life events coinciding with each other, according to how the Lots have fallen such as you are keeping a healthy balance between your work, personal life, love life, health etc. It maybe that you have changed to a more financially stable job which in turn means you can now pay bills correctly, afford to buy healthy or organic foods or socialise more with your friends, or it can mean a number of life issues are weighing you down, and each area needs to be sorted out one by one for the bigger problem to be resolved. The centre can also represent a crossroads in your life in which you have to focus on one area over the other and denote the overall situation/outcome of the reading.

Examples of Readings

Example #1: if the say the key and feather lands on the cross, but a white skull is facing away, this may mean that you are on the right path, but you may need some more advice (guidance) on the matter of your faith in life and desires. Maybe a visit to a trusted friend is on the cards to help refocus you on your path.

Example #2 If the red skull lands on triple circle and the nose is touching the third circle, this means you need to focus on your mental health right now, the things on your mind and stress is getting in the way of what you want to achieve. Maybe taking up meditation, breathing techniques or other wellbeing methods to helps you calmly get through life.

Example #3 if a coin lands on the briefcase but a wish bone and feather in on the graph then it may mean all is going well with work or business bur you wish to have more money. However, the feather on the graph may denote that you need to balance your ingoing's with your outgoing's, or maybe push for that promotion that is long overdue.

Notes

Notes

Notes

Notes

Notes

Notes

Notes

Notes

Printed in Great Britain
by Amazon